ESSENTIALS OF TIME MANAGEMENT
(Taking Control of Your Life)

Shyam Bhatawdekar
Dr Kalpana Bhatawdekar

Essentials of

Time Management

(Taking Control of Your Life)

Books by Shyam Bhatawdekar and Dr Kalpana Bhatawdekar

1. *HSoftware* (Human Software) (The *Only* Key to Higher Effectiveness)
2. Sensitive Stories of Corporate World (Management Case Studies)
3. Classic Management Games, Exercises, Energizers and Icebreakers (Volume 1)
4. Classic Management Games, Exercises, Energizers and Icebreakers (Volume 2)
5. Stress? No Way!! (Handbook on Stress Management)
6. *HSoftware* (Shyam Bhatawdekar's Effectiveness Model)
7. Competencies and Competency Matrix
8. Soft Skills You Can't Do Without (Goal Setting, Time Management, Assertiveness and Anger Management)
9. Essentials of Work Study (Method Study and Work Measurement)
10. Essentials of Time Management (Taking Control of Your Life)
11. Essentials of 5S Housekeeping
12. Essentials of Quality Circles
13. Essentials of Goal Setting
14. Essentials of Anger Management
15. Essentials of Assertive Behavior
16. Essentials of Performance Management & Performance Appraisal
17. Health Essentials (Health Is Wealth)
18. The Romance of Intimacy (How to Enhance Intimacy in a Relationship?)
19. Good People: *Novel, a refreshingly different love story*
20. Funny (and Not So Funny) Short Stories
21. Stories Children Will Love (Volume 1: Bhanu-Shanu-Kaju-Biju and Dholu Ram Gadbad Singh)
22. Travelogue: Scandinavia, Russia

To Our Family

Shyam Bhatawdekar   Dr Kalpana Bhatawdekar

Most people often misunderstand time management. They see it in a very limited sense as synonymous to constructing the timetable of daily or weekly activities and strictly following that schedule. Some sophistication is added to the process by introducing prioritization of activities in deciding the calendar.

But time management is much more than this. In this book it is described as taking control of our life and managing ourselves. It emphasizes on the correct choice of projects, tasks and activities related to your short-term, long-term and lifetime aspirations, objectives and goals.

Therefore, a thorough knowledge of time management in its new avatar becomes imperative. To facilitate gaining the knowledge in this important subject in the shortest possible time, the authors Shyam Bhatawdekar and Dr Kalpana Bhatawdekar included only the appropriate "essentials" of time management in the book.

The authors are top-notch business executives, highly sought after business and management consultants, eminent management gurus, authentic human behavior experts and prolific authors. So the book becomes an authentic document.

To read more by the authors, refer their websites: http://shyam.bhatawdekar.com, *http://writings-of-shyam.blogspot.com* and http://management-universe.blogspot.com

Essentials of Time Management

(Taking Control of Your Life)

**Shyam Bhatawdekar
Dr Kalpana Bhatawdekar**

Published by Publishing Division of

Prodcons Group

8, Pranjal Society, Shiv Tirth Nagar, Paud Road, Pune 411038 (India)

Email: prodcons@prodcons.com

For other web publications, refer: http://management-universe.blogspot.com and http://shyam.bhatawdekar.com

Copyright © with the authors Shyam Bhatawdekar and Dr Kalpana Bhatawdekar

All rights reserved

No reproduction without permission in whole or in part in any form

Contents

1. Time Management = Taking Control of Life- 9
2. Availability of Time: Not an Issue- 10
3. Who Is a Great Time Manager?- 12
4. Peculiar Nature of "Time" Resource- 14
5. Choice of Activities and Prioritization- 15
6. The Process of Time Management- 17
7. Effectiveness and Efficiency: Both Are Important- 19
8. Conflict Between Urgency and Importance- 21
9. Case Study: Doing Important Is Important- 25
10. Another Way of Uncovering Important Tasks- 31
11. Case Study: Prioritization of Unobvious Task- 32
12. Yet Another Way of Uncovering the Important- 37
13. Thus, Time Management Is Five stage Process- 37
14. Procrastination: Thief of Time Management- 38
15. Time Wasters: Another Big Thief- 40
16. Four D's of Time Management- 43
17. You Can't Waste Time in Advance- 45
18. And the Last Suggestion- 46

Essentials of Time Management (Taking Control of Your Life)

Time Management = Taking Control of Life

Show a person who does not want to take control of his life and regulate his life. All the people want it but some kind of confusion surrounds them. They do not know where to begin and what to do.

The confusion gets removed when you remember the following formula:

Life Management = Time Management

Time management encompasses in itself so many secrets which when uncovered become the beacon for taking control of your life.

Therefore understanding time management in its *true sense* is very important. Having understood time management the way it should be understood, you can then start practicing it to your advantage. You will start feeling and seeing that now you have full control over your life.

Peter Drucker, the well-known management author rightly says that until we can manage time, we can manage nothing else. Management of every resource gets impacted by how you carry out your time management.

So get ready to read the most essential aspects of time management (and life management).

Availability of Time: Not an Issue

'I am short of time'. 'Day's 24 hours are not enough for me'. 'Wish I had more time'. 'Time is running out'. 'I can't find enough time for my spouse and children', 'Haven't been on vacation for a long time- no time for that'. These are the various phrases we hear from many people often. But it is not true. Everybody has enough free time after accounting for all the hours one spends on all the essential activities.

Here are the calculations for a typical week:

Total available hours 24 hours X 7 days = 168 hours.
Minus Average sleep 7 hours X 7 days = 49 hours.
Total waking hours = 119 hours.

Average time at office 8 hours X 6 days = 48 hours.

Average time commuting 2 hours X 6 days = 12 hours.

Total work time = 60 hours.

Total work time as % of waking hours 50% approximately.

Free time available after accounting for work time and sleep time = 59 hours.

Total free time as % of waking hours 50% approximately.

So, after carrying out all the essential activities you are left with a big chunk of your time, which is 59 hours a week or approximately 8.4 hours every day. That's really something pretty substantial. This calculation is based on a 6-day workweek. If you take a 5-day workweek you will get an extra bonus of 10 hours a week. This means you get 69 hours a week all for yourself instead of 59 hours.

Time availability, therefore, isn't an issue. Most important thing is "how to use your time and so, how to take control of your time (and therefore, your life)".

Every person has 168 hours a week. What you do with these hours impacts your life in short term as well as long term is the main issue. That determines your effectiveness and efficiency in your life.

Every person can become a great time manager provided he wishes to become one. Desire and will power are vital.

Who Is a Great Time Manager?

You can be called as a great time manager (and a life manager) if you can manage or find time for the activities that are important and essential for you from the ones given below:

- Spouse
- Child/Children
- Family
- Professional work
- Professional networking
- Doing grocery and other purchases
- Fun shopping
- Capital goods purchases
- Introspection and self improvement
- Relationships
- Social networking
- Relaxed meals
- Sleep and relaxation
- Hobbies and interests

- Birthdays, anniversaries and other functions
- Health, exercises and walks
- Games (outdoor and indoor)
- Enjoying the nature
- Reading
- Writing
- Humor and laugh
- Music
- Travel and sightseeing
- Watching few good movies, television programs, concerts and dramas
- Prayer

And any other things that are important to you.

You need time for doing all of this. Where from will you get that kind of time? Answer to this question is the crux of good time management.

We have coined a solution for this and that solution is to create one or two extra months for yourself over and above the 12 months available to you in an year? The person who can do it qualifies to be a good time manager. Since you cannot literally do it what you need to really do is to stop overuse of time in carrying out the activities. You also need to stop wasting your time. Both these actions will result in saving a couple of months every year.

What it also means is to make a prudent choice of activities you will like to perform and to decide on when you will do them and how much time you will like to spend on them. It also means taking a decision on what activities you will not like to perform yourself (though you may delegate or outsource some of them) and what activities you are willing to postpone for the future.

Peculiar Nature of "Time" Resource

Time is a "resource", perhaps the most important resource of existing and emerging scenario. This resource is somewhat different in its nature as compared to the other resources like man, machine, money, material, land and information. It has following peculiarities:

- Time cannot be stored, it cannot be preserved and so it is irretrievable once gone.
- Time is not transferable; it is personal.
- Time is irreversible.

- No rework is possible on time.
- Time itself cannot be sold; therefore it cannot be purchased.
- Every single person on the earth has the same amount of time i.e. 24 hours a day. Person who knows how to use it goes ahead in his life.

Therefore, time is a peculiar resource and needs to be handled differently and more carefully.

In these pages we are trying to help you understand how to tackle this peculiar resource.

Choice of Activities and Prioritization

Time management is all about which activities you should perform and among them which ones you should do on priority basis as compared to others. It also includes decisions on which activities you could outsource and delegate.

Importantly it also includes the decision on which activities need not be done at all. The activities that need not be done at all are essentially the non-value adding activities. Such activities do not add any value of any kind in your personal, professional, family and social life. So doing them using your limited and precious time resource does not make any sense. We call them time wasters. Not doing them does not harm you at all and they do save lots of your precious time.

This now presents to you an uncluttered plate of only the important actions that you need to concentrate on and perform. Since you have removed the clutter, it is easy to focus on the most important activities.

After having chosen the activities to be performed by you or others on your behalf (by way of delegation and outsourcing) it is also important to choose the most efficient processes such that they consume various required resources in the most optimal way. One of the important resources to consider is the "time" resource. You should aim at an overall optimization resulting in overall economy, better quality of the outcome and meeting the time line.

If you want an answer on which activity you must perform at this moment, your time management should be able to guide you by saying, "Do this activity now over the next so much time. Then take up the next activity that starts at such and such time." If you can get this kind of answer from your time management, your time management is perfect.

Therefore, in order to strive for a perfect time management you must keep asking this question frequently, "What is the best use of my time right now?"

To attain this kind of perfection in your time management you should follow the process of time management given below. Implementing the correct process will result in the best advantages from your time management for you.

The Process of Time Management

The process should be followed in the sequence as given below:

1. Work out goals for a chosen period (or if possible, work our lifetime goals). The chosen period could be say, next one year or next three years or five years (those who can visualize their goals for the entire period of their life can attempt to work out their lifetime goals).
2. Resolve goal conflicts.

3. Set priorities.
4. Select your top three or four goals.
5. List all the tasks and the activities to be performed for achieving each of the chosen three or four goals.
6. Identify interdependence and sequence of the activities. Resolve conflict between urgent and important tasks or activities.
7. Set priorities to allow you to select the most effective activities to do now and to do later during the day and the week. Thus you land up with the timetable of performing the various activities.
8. So now you can prepare "weekly to do list" and then "daily to do" list and their timetable.
9. Act as per priority activities thus chosen.
10. Choose the most efficient ways or processes to accomplish the task or activities.
11. Move on to the next priority tasks and activities week after week and day after day and so on till you achieve your goals.

If you strictly follow the above-mentioned process of time management it will always answer the question: "What is the best use of my time now? Which activity I must perform at this instant?" You have prepared a ready reckoner timetable of each day and each week in this way.

Effectiveness or Efficiency: Both Are Important

By choosing the right kind of goal oriented jobs or tasks (i.e. the ones that are important to accomplish your goals) you have already become effective.

Now you have to become efficient too. Choosing the right processes or methods to carry out your chosen tasks and activities will do this (refer step number 10 of the process of time management described in earlier paragraph).

However honest and sincere you are, there is no point in carrying out any work endlessly and seeking a deceptive satisfaction of working hard. Rather work smart by choosing the best process. Exercise due care in selecting the methods, processes and tools.

We can illustrate this point by taking one simple example. Say, you wish to cut a tree by a hacksaw or by a power saw. For doing this you must first make sure to sharpen the teeth of the saw. If you attempt to start on the job with a blunt saw thinking that you would save time that goes into sharpening the saw, you are terribly mistaken. Using a blunt saw will only result in enormously large amount of time to cut the tree or in the worst case the tree will not be felled at all despite your getting horrendously tired by the sheer hard work you put in.

More prudent thing will be to take some time out and sharpen the saw. Since the saw is sharpened, you are now using the right kind of tool. The tree will be felled within no time without getting tired. That's some smart work! And that's what we call efficiency. So now you are effective as well as efficient- two vital aspects of good time management.

Another example that comes to mind when we talk of choosing the right processes is to investing some time on maintenance of the system(s) using which you get the outputs- maintenance of production machines, maintenance of computer systems, maintenance of one's mind and body etc.

Do *right* activities *rightly* for effectiveness and efficiency.

Conflict Between Urgency and Importance

On prioritizing the activities most people often make mistake between choosing:

- "Urgent and important tasks" and
- "Important but not urgent tasks"

They are often guided by the obvious. The obvious is "urgent and important tasks". Therefore they choose to carry out the urgent and important tasks first. And since these tasks have become urgent and delaying them any further can be very costly or fatal, their decision seems to be correct in the first analysis.

And since the tasks have become urgent, it is like an emergency situation, a fire-fighting situation. Tackling such situations often demands far more time and other resources and leaves the performers highly stressed. Tackling the urgencies, emergencies and fire-fighting repeatedly can be dangerous.

So a second analysis is warranted.

Ask a question: "Why in the first place this task became urgent?"

The answer will suggest that this task was not started on time or it took more time to do than expected. Every task has a definite lead-time or cycle time to complete. So you must start the task well in advance of its desired completion date considering its lead-time or cycle time and allowing for contingencies that might creep in during its execution.

At times a task can become urgent if the activity/activities on which it is dependent or interdependent might not have been done. For example your car may breakdown while driving and now fixing it up becomes urgent because you did not carry out the preventive maintenance of the car in time or properly. It surely will cost more money and develop stress.

The ideal situation is when you have no urgencies or fire fighting and every important task is carried out in a normal way by starting it well in time. It requires a good amount of planning. Thus in essence planning and prioritizing are the keys to good time management.

The foregoing discussion indicates that we should be guided by the following sequence in terms of prioritizing the tasks or activities:

Priority 1:

"Important but not urgent tasks" (If you take these as your top priority, the urgent tasks will minimize. As urgency minimizes, your stress levels and excessive expenditure of time and other resources will also come down. For example: though maintaining your health is very important yet, even if you do not take steps to upkeep it on a regular basis, it will not deteriorate suddenly today or tomorrow. Therefore maintaining health, though important, cannot be classified as an urgent task. So if you keep on ignoring it for a long period considering it as not urgent and do not take care of it in time, at some later date you may land up with a very bad health situation. At that time it would have become urgent all of a sudden).

Priority 2:

"Urgent and important tasks" (You will have to take them up as priority since they have become urgent for whatever reasons. But you should try to minimize instances of such tasks by concentrating on "important but not urgent tasks" early on before they slide down to becoming urgent. For example: maintaining relationships with customers, which is an important task, if not carried out over a period of time and properly may result in cancelled orders presenting an organizational crisis. Attending to a breakdown of an important machine becomes urgent but you could have avoided this kind of urgency and firefighting by carrying out its preventive maintenance in time as a priority).

Priority 3:

"Urgent but not important tasks" (These are good candidates for delegation and outsourcing. Do not spend your time and your other resources on them).

Priority 4:

"Not important and not urgent tasks" (Examine these tasks carefully. You may find that these may also include non-value adding or wasteful activities. You may as well decide not to perform such activities at all. You can safely dump them without any fear).

Since prioritization of tasks based on the guidelines specified above is very important, we are elaborating it by presenting a case study here.

Case Study: Doing Important Is Important

Peter Gonzales was quite a frustrated soul. His organization had a funny rule. It denied promotions to the levels of 'manager' and upwards in its technical departments to any person who was not an engineering graduate even if the person was competent.

Peter Gonzales had stopped his studies after getting a diploma in mechanical engineering. He had believed all along that his industry and hard work could take him to places despite his modest formal qualifications. He never imagined that his lack of education would come in way of his promotions to higher levels in the hierarchy of the company he was working for.

Around this time when Peter Gonzales was highly frustrated, this company contracted us (the authors of this book) for an assignment of mentorship to the employees of the company. So, he was one of our earlier subjects to mentor.

"Thrice my boss has recommended me to the position of 'manager' based on my performance appraisal but every time it has been rejected. The HR department puts forth the rule book of the company and my case gets sidelined," Peter poured out his heart to us in our first meeting.

He told us that he had even contemplated leaving the organization but it was not easy to get another decent job in that region due to paucity of industrial firms in that region. Plus he had some family compulsions. His ailing old father and mother used to stay in a nearby town and he was required to be around to take care of them. So, he preferred to stay in the township of the company that was close by to the town where his parents resided.

Thus, in a way his fate was sealed if he had to continue in this organization. He won't get the promotion he wanted so badly. So did he really have a choice? Should he retire at the existing position or do something about it?

After considerable discussion with him, we proposed to him, "If your formal qualifications are coming in way of your progress, why don't you think of getting an engineering degree by joining an evening course in a nearby engineering college or join a distance learning program that might be available somewhere."

He had thought about it but there was no engineering college in that region and only distance course available was AMIE (that was considered equivalent of an engineering degree and was also recognized by his organization).

However, as per Peter, AMIE was a very tough course and needed one to work very hard and he would have to pursue it without much guidance from anyone. It needed lots of spare time too- that was most important requirement for completing AMIE. Now that he was a family man with a wife and two kids and they took most of his time away, he just could not take up AMIE course.

We said, "We agree with you. For every person, time has always been a constraint. No one has unlimited time at one's disposal. But if one can do a good 'time management', it was possible to find out time particularly for those activities that are important in one's life. Many people spend lots of their time on unimportant activities and thus do not find time to do the important activities."

Peter became a bit defensive, "Do you mean to say that I while away my time on unimportant activities? After coming home from office I have scores of errands to attend to. I need to do grocery, go to bank, go to post office, attend parent-teacher meetings in the kids' schools and so on. Are they not important jobs? And we need to do a bit of socializing too- after all we are living in this small township and we need to maintain relationships with our co- dwellers."

We enquired, "But all of this cannot consume your entire evening. And why don't you train your wife to do most of these things? She can surely handle all these jobs on her own with a little bit of handholding in the beginning but will become quite independent after some time. Then you will have good amount of time for your AMIE studies."

Hearing this, Peter did some mental calculations and said, "But we also spend some family time together watching television- the only entertainment in this township."

We got curious and asked, "How much TV do you watch every day?"

His reply shocked us, "At least 3 to 4 hours every night- that means at least one or two movies a day."

We argued, "But that's an overdose of entertainment by any standard. If you insist on watching so much of TV and indulge in so much of entertainment, you can be satisfied with the success story of entertaining yourself throughout your life but we can give you in writing that you will retire only as an 'assistant manager' while all of your colleagues will climb the hierarchical ladder. You may not like that situation."

We added further, "More than that, your wife and kids will not like being left behind. You are still very young, just about 35 years and you have another at least 25 years of professional career. So think about cutting down on your entertainment and easily save 3 to 4 hours of you precious time. Use that for completing AMIE. It's just a matter of 2 to 3 years. After you achieve AMIE, do spend some of your time in entertaining yourself."

Our constructive criticism worked positively on him. He realized that doing AMIE was by far the most important thing in his life at that juncture. For this, he felt convinced that he needed adequate time to study the various difficult courses of AMIE. He understood that he could manage this time for himself for AMIE by training his wife to do the chores like bank, post office, grocery, parent-teacher meets, socializing etc thus delegating all of this work to her. They could cut down on watching TV thus freeing all of them to divert their attention to more important things in life.

He wrote to us later that he had finally enrolled himself for AMIE course. After a gap of around 3 years, we got a phone call from Peter Gonzales that he completed AMIE successfully, got promoted to the position of 'manager' and the company had allotted him a higher category of house in the township.

We congratulated him on his excellent demonstration of "time management" in action.

Another Way of Uncovering Important Tasks

At times you come across situations when you miss out visualizing the important tasks of your personal and professional life. Missing them out on your agenda of important task results in their exclusion from the list of your priority activities. This ultimately results in not achieving some important goals. And who wants a situation like this?

Therefore we suggest a deliberate attempt on your part to unearth such important tasks of your life that have escaped your mind till date. For this ask the following question:

"What are those few tasks and activities that I did not undertake till date, if I undertake them now onwards will make significant positive difference or advancement in my professional and personal life?"

Well thought-out answers to this question will help in surfacing or uncovering those few very important tasks that you must now include as your top priority tasks. Accomplishing such tasks will ensure your growth and advancement in personal and professional life.

Since this topic is of great value-addition to a large number of people, we cite here a case study to help understand this topic better.

Case Study: Prioritization of Unobvious Task

Around twenty vice presidents and general managers of a well known large company in the corporate sector were attentively listening to our concluding remarks in the two days seminar on "time management". We (authors of this book) were telling them that time management was not about accounting the hours and minutes of one's day or doing all kinds of activities with the aim of minimizing the time taken on them but it was all about how well one spent his time on the objectives, projects, tasks and activities that were most important to him.

To help them understand this concept better, we left them with a question, the answer to which would uncover their most important objectives and related activities. We advised them to answer the question with lots of thinking. The question was: "What couple of things could you do (which you are not doing now or are not doing them seriously) that if you did them persistently, would make a tremendous difference in your personal and professional life?"

We left them at that.

Then, we got busy with our other clients for the next few months. We also used to frequently visit the above-mentioned company on our various consulting assignments there.

On one such occasion when we were on a visit to this company for consultations and after a hectic meeting were relaxing a bit in its board room, a gentleman knocked at the door, opened it slightly, looked at us enquiringly and said, "Excuse me, can I see you for a while? I won't take much of your time though."

We said, "Please come and have a seat."

He mentioned without wasting much of time, "I was one of the participants of your very first time management seminar you conducted for the top and the senior managers of our company a few months ago. I was quite influenced by your seminar. Now, implementing what you told hugely benefited me and I wish to share that with you. Can I take a lift in your car in the evening so that I can tell you in detail all about it?"

We said, "It suits us, you are most welcome." Then we got busy for the rest of the day.

After finishing our job that day, as we were about to get into our car, that gentleman was already there waiting for me. We let him in. We drove the car out of the company premises and as we were on the main road, he started talking. He was quite enthusiastic about what he spoke.

He said, "First of all, I wish to thank you both from the bottom of my heart. You literally changed my life. Had I not uncovered my real love I would have been doomed."

Then, he proceeded to tell us his entire story, "I was not very happy with what I was doing all along. The shop floor job never suited me. Yet I continued with it. With my intelligence and hard work, it was not difficult for me to succeed even in that kind of shop floor oriented production job that I really detested badly. I got promotions pretty fast but frankly I wasn't just cut out for it intellectually."

"Something was seriously missing. Outwardly everything looked fine to me and to others because I was a fast promoted person to the extent that I am one of the youngest general managers in the company. But inwardly, I knew I was not comfortable."

He paused and continued again, "And then, I heard your talk on time management and particularly the question you gave us to answer towards the conclusion of the seminar. It haunted me for a few days. I started looking at it and understanding it with lots of seriousness. I started finding its answer and one day it occurred to me that I should switch over to a job that is closer to my heart and mind."

He continued speaking, "I asked myself- what is that? The answer was staring at me; I needed a job, which would use my analytical, systems and management skills. Also the job should provide me with better career progression. What was it?"

"I went on playing with many answers and finally zeroed in on ERP (enterprise resource planning) as my new area of action. Once I was clear about it, I hurried up and took a three months evening course on ERP and on one specific

ERP package in one of the most reputed institutes. It was an expensive program and yet, I was happy investing the amount."

"Luckily, my existing company is already going ahead implementing ERP and knowing that I am a qualified ERP professional offered me to head the new ERP department. I have already accepted the offer and started the ERP implementation work in the company. I am really enjoying every minute of my time now. I feel as if it is the start of a new life for me, full of rewards that I like. I sincerely wish to thank you. You and your time management program changed my life. Thanks."

We had reached his home and he got down from the car. We drove away the car in the direction of our home feeling once more convinced that if one understands time management in its true sense it works.

Time management is all about prioritizing life's important tasks even if they are not quite obvious in the first or at times, even in the second analysis.

Yet Another Way of Uncovering the Important

There is yet another very potent way of uncovering your important projects and their related tasks and activities.

Imagine you are going to live just for today and no more.

If that is the scenario then what are the things you will like to take care of before you are no more on this earth tomorrow. This will expose to you the stark reality of what are the most important things for you in your life.

Study what surfaces from this harsh scenario. Then examine the things that emerged as important and try to include them in your priority list.

Spending your precious time on trivia is a waste.

Thus, Time Management Is Five Stage Process

1. *Planning:* Goal setting/target setting, prioritizing the goals.

2. *Activity analysis:* Selection of activities, eliminating or minimizing non-optimal/non-value adding activities.
3. *Prioritizing the activities and scheduling:* Their sequencing, preparing activity network and putting them on a time line.
4. *Resource organization:* Plan out and position the required resources (including time).
5. *Execution, review and correction:* Carry out the activities, review them on a planned basis and incorporate corrections and modifications to ensure timely and economic completion.

Procrastinating: Thief of Time Management

Procrastination or postponing tasks or activities screws up the time management. Let us examine this phenomenon of procrastination in some details. Once we understand it, we can take necessary steps to avoid procrastination as given later in this section.

Why Do We Procrastinate?

Two major reasons to procrastinate certain tasks are their:

- Boredom and
- Fear

Areas of Procrastination

- Difficult people
- Boring tasks
- Risky/unfamiliar work
- Difficult phone calls
- Large projects
- Public contacts
- Small tasks

Select two of your most problematic areas from the above list and focus your attention on them over next few weeks.

How Do We Procrastinate?

- Small versus large (It's too small a job, I will do it later. Its too large a job, I will do it later.)
- Perfectionist (Postpone to a more conducive time)
- Waste of time (Oh, its waste of time doing this work)

- Phoning at lunch (so that the person at the other end is not available and you escape from doing the work which you really want to procrastinate)
- Avoiding the task (unpleasant, boring, lack of expertise, dealing with difficult party)

Action Plan for Less Procrastination

- Commit yourself to start times.
- Break large projects down into manageable portions.
- Control the amount of paper and e-communication.
- Prioritize your tasks.
- Reward yourself: Give yourself a deadline and then plan a treat when you reach it. This will give you something to look forward to.

Time Wasters: Another Big Thief

A large number of people waste unimaginably large chunks of their valuable time on wasteful activities. These activities include all "non-value adding activities" and "not important and not urgent tasks".

We give below a list of various types of time wasters, which are commonly observed. You may add your own to the list and make the list more comprehensive. Then check if you are victims of how many of them. Also try to put down the time you loose by indulging in those time wasters.

Self-Discipline

- Never make daily or weekly to-do lists
- Never set my goals/deadlines
- Set goals/deadlines and don't stick to them
- Wander around and interrupt others for a chat
- Low level of concentration, easily distracted
- Try to do more than one thing at once
- Get involved in everything
- Make social calls regularly

Can't Say No

- Like to help others
- Like to feel important
- Fear of upsetting people
- I always say yes
- Constantly interrupted
- Accept unrealistic deadlines
- Cannot get rid of callers or visitors quickly
- Drop what I'm doing to deal with non-urgent queries

Bogged Down

- Can't delegate

- Involved in everything
- Too much paper, too much e-communication
- Poor administration routines
- Forget things
- Badly organized
- Too much routine work
- No system for reading
- Messy environment
- Slow at writing letters and reports
- Lengthy unstructured telephone calls
- No systems for controlling telephone conversations

Badly Run Meetings (including one-to-one)

- No agenda or timeline
- No clear objective agreed at the start
- Wrong people
- Stray off the subject
- Can't get my point of view across
- People don't listen
- No conclusions or actions
- Badly chaired
- Negative attitudes

Systems And Procedures

- Untidy work
- Forget things
- Messages not passed on/received
- Don't file regularly
- Don't know managers' daily/weekly priorities
- Don't know who does what in other departments
- Always looking for things
- Don't know whose work to do first

Poor Communication

- I only think about it after the event
- We are unaware of each other's needs for information
- Other departments don't seem interested in my problems
- Never get an answer
- We all have different priorities
- Haven't got the time to communicate
- Assume that people understand my motives

Identify the time wasters that apply to you. Concentrate on the ones that waste maximum of your time. Take actions.

Four D's of Time Management

In an earlier paragraph we specified the guidelines of prioritization of the tasks. As per those guidelines you are expected to take up the "important tasks (though not urgent)" as the first priority and "urgent (and important) tasks" as your equally important priority. However you come across many tasks that creep in between these high priority tasks. So we must set out some more guidelines to tackle such tasks.

These guidelines are given below:

Do it now:

If the interrupting task takes less time say just up to 10 minutes, do it right away and get done with it. Concentrate on it while doing it. The examples of such tasks are: attending a telephone call, reading a note or an email of some importance, listening to a person who thinks he needs to speak with you urgently etc.

Dump it, discard it or delete it:

Decide if the task really needs to be done. If the task is non-value adding, unimportant and not urgent, you can dump it. If the tasks do not contribute towards accomplishments of your objectives or goals, there is no point wasting your time on them. You need not have to feel guilty of dumping such activities. Be ruthless towards them.

Delegate it:

The tasks, which may be urgent but not important enough for you to do them yourself, should be delegated to your colleagues/direct reports or outsourced. To delegate effectively, you need to know the strengths and weaknesses of those who can be delegated. You should also assess if the person whom you wish to delegate will enjoy doing that task.

Defer it:

If you need to do the task yourself but it is going to take longer than 10 minutes, defer it. Often tasks that were not planned show up and obviously you've not allocated time to attend to them. Examine such tasks to check if they are not the ones which require earlier mentioned 3 D's i.e. do it now, dump it or delegate it. If they are outside of these 3 D's, you can safely defer them. Include them in your next set of plan i.e. deciding when the particular tasks should be picked up again for your attention.

You Can't Waste Time in Advance

This point holds a very important lesson to learn. And that is- howsoever badly you might have goofed on your time management in the past, the time that will be available to you from this moment onwards for your entire future is still intact, uncorrupted and full in quantity, as much as all of others will have.

So learn time management right now and apply it properly from now on. If you feel that you wasted your time in the past, you just have no power to waste the time that you have for your future. Your future still remains spotless. You lost nothing much; you can still make up for it and still go further.

You still have the power to plan out your tomorrow. Use all the good time management principles and reshape rest of your life on personal, family, professional and social fronts. Your second, third and many more innings can still be brilliant.

And its not too late either since tomorrow is just a day away from now.

And the Last Suggestion

It is not important how many hours you work but it is important to ask how much of yourself you put into it during that period in a smart way, the "time management" way. Leaders do it themselves and enthuse their people and organization to do it.

www.ingramcontent.com/pod-product-compliance
Lightning Source LLC
Chambersburg PA
CBHW061520180526
45171CB00001B/265